D0516046

DISCARDED FROM
GARFIELD COUNTY PUBLIC
LIBRARY SYSTEM

Garfield County Libraries
Glenwood Springs Branch
413 9th Street
Glenwood Springs, CO 81601
(970) 945-5958 · Fax (970) 945-7723
www.GCPLD.org

Life's Challenges

GOOD-BYE, JEEPERS

What to Expect When Your Pet Dies

by Nancy Loewen

illustrated by
Christopher Lyles

PICTURE WINDOW BOOKS
a capstone imprint

One Saturday morning, I poured my cereal. I poured my milk. Then I stopped.

Something was missing.

Usually, the rustling of the cereal bag made Jeepers squeak. Jeepers was my guinea pig. He squeaked whenever he heard the crinkling sound of plastic bags. He thought he was getting a treat.

I rustled the cereal bag again. Nothing.

I went to Jeepers's cage and lifted up his hut. He was curled into a ball.
His eyes were open ... but he wasn't seeing me.

"Mom! Dad!" I yelled. **"Something's wrong with Jeepers!"**

I ran into my room. After a few minutes
Dad came in. **"I'm sorry, buddy,"**
he said, **"but Jeepers is—"**

"Dead," I said. **"I know.
I'm not a baby."**

My lips felt funny all of a sudden.

"It's OK to cry," Dad said, putting his arm around
me. **"It might make you feel better."**

But I pressed my lips together. I didn't want to cry.

At first, you might pretend that your pet hasn't died, or that you don't care. That's OK. But so is crying right away. There is no right or wrong way to act when a pet dies. Grief is different for everyone.

I was so glad when the doorbell rang. I didn't want to think about death and all that sad stuff. Anton and his cousin asked me to go to the playground with them. So I did.

We went down the spiral slide 10 times.

We hung upside down from the monkey bars and played tic-tac-toe in the sand.

I hardly thought about Jeepers at all.

Grief isn't a single feeling. It can be many feelings that come and go over time. And it's OK to think of things other than your pet. It's even OK to have fun! It doesn't mean that you didn't love your pet.

When I got home, Mom was wrapping a shoebox with gold foil. The foil made a crinkling sound, like a cereal bag. **"Later this afternoon we'll take Jeepers to Aunt Judy's house,"** she said. **"We can bury him in her yard."**

My lips started feeling funny again.

"You know, honey, Jeepers was pretty old, for a guinea pig," Mom said.

When your pet dies, you might feel guilty. You might think that if you'd done a better job caring for your pet, he or she wouldn't have died. That's a common feeling.

"So it wasn't my fault?" I asked. I thought about the times I'd forgotten to give Jeepers fresh water.

Mom hugged me. "No, Jeepers had a good life here, with all of us. I'll miss him."

"I'll miss him too!" I burst out, and we both started to cry.

9

After Mom and I were done crying,
we made Jeepers the coolest box ever.

We lined the box with a comfy towel.
Mom took Jeepers out of his cage
and carefully set him inside. At first I
didn't want to touch him. But then I
did. His body was cool and stiff, but
his fur still felt as soft as ever.

On the bus to Aunt Judy's house, a lady across the aisle smiled at me. **"That sure is a beautiful box,"** she said. **"You must be carrying something very special in there."**

I didn't feel like smiling back.

"Our pet guinea pig died," Mom explained. "We're taking him out to my sister's yard to bury him."

"I'm very sorry for your loss," the lady said to me in a kind voice.

Suddenly everyone was looking at my gold box.

"What was his name?" a girl asked.

"Jeepers," I replied.

"Could he do any tricks?" a boy asked.

Talking about your pet is a way of honoring him or her. You'll feel better, remembering the good times and knowing that your pet won't be forgotten.

"Not really," I said. "But he could squeak louder than anything."

"Once he squeaked so loudly I thought the smoke alarm was going off!" Dad said.

Everyone around us laughed. I smiled a little.

"I used to have a guinea pig named Patches," the boy said. "I had to be careful or she'd nibble my hair."

"Hey, I had a dog named Patches!" the girl said.

Death is a part of living. We can't avoid it. Everyone has, or will have, experiences with death. It's one of the things that draws us closer together.

A man with a hat put down his newspaper. **"My cat, Pickles, used to sleep on my head,"** he said.

By the time we reached our stop, it seemed like the whole bus knew about Jeepers. And we'd heard stories of all sorts of awesome pets.

When I got off the bus, I still felt sad. But not as sad as before.

I waved good-bye as the bus rolled away.

And then we buried Jeepers.

Pets that have died might be buried in yards or pet cemeteries. They might be cremated, and their ashes scattered in a special place. Treating your pet's body with care and respect can be an important part of saying good-bye.

That night our apartment felt so empty.
It felt that way for a long time.

Sometimes I forgot that Jeepers was gone. In the morning, I'd rustle the cereal bag and listen for his squeak.

After school, I'd save him the last bite of my apple.

My teacher, Mr. Dennis, and I talked about Jeepers a lot. Mr. Dennis
is a little goofy, but he's a good listener. He used to have a pet tarantula
when he was a kid. He knows what it feels like when a pet dies.

21

Mom and Dad told me that when I was ready, I could get another pet.

"How will I know when I'm ready?" I asked.

"You'll know," Mom said. **"It's when you think about Jeepers and feel happy that you knew him, instead of sad that you lost him."**

I hope that time comes soon. This place is way too quiet.

Glossary

cemetery—a place where people or animals are buried; a graveyard

cremate—to expose a body to high heat, which turns it into ash

grief—the process we go through when we experience death or another kind of loss; when we grieve, we might feel sadness, anger, loneliness, and other emotions

guilty—a feeling of having done something wrong; feeling shame

honor—to show respect for someone or something

Read More

Cochran, Bill. *The Forever Dog*. New York: HarperCollins, 2007.

Cohen, Miriam. *Jim's Dog, Muffins*. New York: Star Bright Books, 2008.

Rylant, Cynthia. *Cat Heaven*. New York: Blue Sky Press, 1997.

Rylant, Cynthia. *Dog Heaven*. New York: Blue Sky Press, 1995.

Internet Sites

FactHound offers a safe, fun way to find Internet sites related to this book. All of the sites on FactHound have been researched by our staff.

Here's all you do:

Visit *www.facthound.com*

Type in this code: 9781404866805

Super-cool stuff! Check out projects, games and lots more at **www.capstonekids.com**

Index

Look for all the books in the Life's Challenges series:

Good-bye, Jeepers

The Night Dad Went to Jail

Saying Good-bye to Uncle Joe

Weekends with Dad

Thanks to our advisers for their expertise, research, and advice:

Michele Goyette-Ewing, PhD
Director of Psychology Training
Yale Child Study Center

Terry Flaherty, PhD
Professor of English
Minnesota State University, Mankato

Editor: Jill Kalz
Designer: Alison Thiele
Art Director: Nathan Gassman
Production Specialist: Sarah Bennett
The illustrations in this book were created with collage and enhanced digitally.

Picture Window Books
151 Good Counsel Drive
P.O. Box 669
Mankato, MN 56002-0669
877-845-8392
www.capstonepub.com

Copyright © 2012 by Picture Window Books, a Capstone imprint.
All rights reserved. No part of this book may be reproduced without
written permission from the publisher. The publisher takes no
responsibility for the use of any of the materials or methods described
in this book, nor for the products thereof.

All books published by Picture Window Books
are manufactured with paper containing at least
10 percent post-consumer waste.

Library of Congress Cataloging-in-Publication Data
Loewen, Nancy, 1964–
  Good-bye, Jeepers : what to expect when your pet dies /
by Nancy Loewen ; illustrated by Christopher Lyles.
    p. cm. — (Life's challenges)
  ISBN 978-1-4048-6680-5 (library binding)
  1. Pet owners—Psychology—Juvenile literature. 2.
Pets—Death—Psychological aspects—Juvenile literature. 3.
Bereavement—Psychological aspects—Juvenile literature. 4. Children
and animals—Juvenile literature. 5. Children and death—Juvenile
literature. I. Lyles, Christopher, 1977– II. Title. III. Series.

SF411.47.L64 2012
155.9'37—dc22
                             2011007455

Printed in the United States of America in North Mankato, Minnesota.
032011   006110CGF11